FACING TRAGEDY
on the TITANIC

A HISTORY SEEKING ADVENTURE

by Allison Lassieur

CAPSTONE PRESS

a capstone imprint

Published by You Choose, an imprint of Capstone
1710 Roe Crest Drive, North Mankato, Minnesota 56003
capstonepub.com

Library of Congress Cataloging-in-Publication Data is available on the Library of
Congress website.

ISBN: 9781669058182 (hardcover)
ISBN: 9781669058151 (paperback)
ISBN: 9781669058168 (ebook PDF)

Summary: YOU have found yourself aboard the ill-fated RMS *Titanic*. Where you
find yourself when the ship strikes the deadly iceberg and the decisions you make
afterward will mean the difference between life and death. Step back in time to
make the difficult choices that real people made in the face of this historic tragedy.

Editorial Credits
Editor: Mandy Robbins; Designer: Heidi Thompson; Media Researcher: Jo Miller;
Production Specialist: Tori Abraham

Image Credits
Alamy: Chronicle, 28, Colin Waters, 33, GG Archives, 97, Niday Picture Library,
48, PA Images, 56, United Archives GmbH, 78; Getty Images: Albert Harlingue,
44, Bettmann, 65, Hulton Collection, 63, Popperfoto, 106, Roger Viollet, 19,
Topical Press Agency, 9; Library of Congress, 54, 105; Newscom: akg-images, 95;
Science Source: Patrick Landmann, 60, SPL, 13; Shutterstock: Everett Collection,
Cover, 22, 70, posteriori, 58, WindVector, 4; Superstock: Universal Images, 35

All internet sites appearing in back matter were available and accurate when this
book was sent to press.

Printed and bound in China. 5592

TABLE OF CONTENTS

About Your Adventure.....................5

CHAPTER 1
Countdown to Disaster....................7

CHAPTER 2
Working on the Ship of Dreams............ 11

CHAPTER 3
All Hands on Deck.......................43

CHAPTER 4
Every Man for Himself 75

CHAPTER 5
After the Disaster 101

Titanic Timeline................... 106
Other Paths to Explore............. 108
Bibliography 109
Glossary 110
Read More 111
Internet Sites.................... 111
About the Author..................112

Spot where RMS *TITANIC* sank

NORTH ATLANTIC OCEAN

Ireland

United Kingdom

APRIL 15, 1912

Portugal

Azores

ABOUT YOUR ADVENTURE

YOU are about to live through the most famous ocean disaster in history. On the night of April 14, 1912, the horrible event unfolded. It was a black night with calm, cold seas. The world's most luxurious ocean liner was on its maiden voyage. Then disaster struck.

The RMS *Titanic*, a ship that had been touted as unsinkable, hit an iceberg and sank. Of the 2,240 people on board, the ship took more than 1,500 to their deaths. Will you be one of them?

Turn the page to begin your adventure.

CHAPTER 1

COUNTDOWN TO DISASTER

A few minutes before midnight on April 14, 1912, the RMS *Titanic* was steaming through the freezing cold Atlantic. It was a clear night, so clear that the captain and the officers were confident that the lookouts would see any icebergs in their path. But that was not the case. The ship struck an iceberg that tore her hull.

For the next two hours, the ocean liner slowly sank. There were only 20 lifeboats—not nearly enough to save everyone.

Turn the page.

Only about 700 passengers and crew escaped. Survivors were mostly first-class passengers, but they also included other passengers and people who lived and worked on the ship. Depending on where a person worked or stayed on the ship, they may have had a better or worse chance of survival. Even so, every choice that a survivor made allowed them to live when so many others did not.

Do you think you would have made the right choices on that cold, deadly night? Step into the past aboard this legendary vessel. Experience her grandness and put yourself in the shoes of those who lived through this unimaginable disaster.

- To be a first-class stewardess, turn to page 11.
- To be a seasoned ship's officer, turn to page 43.
- To be a second-class passenger, turn to page 75.

Titanic during its construction in Harland and Wolff's shipyard, Belfast, Ireland

CHAPTER 2

WORKING ON THE SHIP OF DREAMS

You are the oldest child in a large family in London, England. When you were thirteen years old, your father died. Your mother got a job as a stewardess on a small mail ship. You stayed home and watched your younger siblings while your mom sent money home. When you were old enough, you became a ship's stewardess too, leaving the childcare to your younger sister. You weren't sure if you would like life at sea. Now, you can't imagine being anywhere else.

Turn the page.

A ship stewardess has many jobs. It's your responsibility to make beds, vacuum carpets, and dust furniture. You are also expected to answer questions, run errands, and perform other tasks at your passengers' requests. It's hard work, but you get to travel a lot.

One day, you hear the thrilling news that the White Star Line is building the world's largest and grandest ship—the RMS *Titanic*. You decide to apply for a stewardess job on the *Titanic*, and you are accepted!

The new crew members must board before the passengers arrive. You should find your own cabin and settle in. But you'd also like to locate your friend Joe, who works as a cook in the first-class galley, or kitchen.

- To find your cabin, go to the next page.
- To search for Joe, turn to page 24.

While the ship was being built, the architect, Thomas Andrews, asked the employees how he could make the *Titanic* more comfortable for them. As you head to your cabin, you look around to see if he took anyone's advice. To your delight, he did! For instance, crew cabins are often cramped and dark. But the *Titanic's* employee cabins are large, with separate bunks and small wardrobes to store clothing.

Thomas Andrews

Turn the page.

You find your cabin and meet Anne, your roommate. You and Anne unpack and decorate the cabin with family photos and souvenirs from your travels. Then Anne suggests you explore the ship before passengers arrive.

Soon, you and Anne find the first-class cabins. You've never seen such luxuriousness in your life! The largest cabins have their own bathrooms, servants' quarters, and a private deck that overlooks the ocean. As you climb the Grand Staircase, with its beautiful glass-domed ceiling, you hear voices. It's Captain Smith himself! He's with John Jacob Astor, one of the world's richest men. The young woman on his arm must be his new wife, Madeline.

At noon, the ship's whistle blows, alerting everyone that the *Titanic* is about to sail. You and Anne return to your assigned areas. You know it will take a few days to settle into a routine, but you're looking forward to it.

By Sunday, April 14, things are going well. As with other days, today is filled with a whirl of cleaning, running errands, answering questions, and any other chores. By the end of your shift, you're exhausted but still glad to be working on this magnificent ship.

Every evening, you unwind with a stroll along the deck. You love looking at the night sky, full of so many stars. It's no different tonight, although it's quite cold. You cut your walk short because of the chill and are soon asleep in your warm bunk.

You are wakened from your slumber by a splash and a scream. When you turn on the light, you see Anne standing in a foot of water with a terrified look on her face.

"What is happening?" she cries. "Is the ship sinking?"

Turn the page.

"That's not possible!" you say. "But we have to find out what's going on."

Quickly, you dress and grab life belts, just in case. You can't understand why no one woke you up! The hallway is strangely empty. Your heart begins to pound in fear. You can't help but wonder if you're having a bad dream.

As you head down the hall, you hear a baby's cry.

"Surely it's with its mother," you say. But what if the child is lost? Do you check on the child or go up to the deck to find out what's happening?

- To find the child, go to the next page.
- To find out what's going on, turn to page 20.

The cries are coming from a nearby cabin. When you peek in, you see the baby and two other children huddled in fear.

"Where is your mother?" you ask. Neither child replies. You assume they don't speak English.

You take the crying baby, and Anne pulls the older children up. It's slower going with the kids in tow, but you eventually make your way to the boat deck, your heart pounding. You're hoping for good news. The ship can't be sinking, can it?

People crowd the decks near the lifeboats.

"Women and children only!" yells the deckhand loading the boat.

You stop the first steward you see and demand to know what's going on.

"She hit an iceberg," he says, almost shouting. "We're going down."

Turn the page.

You barely have time to process this news when an officer takes the baby from your arms and hands it into a lifeboat. The two other children go next. Since you are a woman, you assume they will let you in the lifeboat. But the officer puts his hand up at you and Anne.

"Sorry. You're employees," he says, shaking his head. "Only passengers."

You stare in disbelief as the last lifeboat is lowered without you. You and Anne cling to one another in terror as you watch waves wash up on the deck. One by one, you watch people lose their footing, scream, and grab at anything they can. Suddenly, something hits you from behind, tearing you out of Anne's arms. It's the last thing you remember as you're swallowed into the sea.

THE END

To follow another path, turn to page 8.
To learn what happened after *Titanic* sank, turn to page 101.

Passengers strolling on deck before *Titanic* hit the iceberg

"You take care of this," you tell Anne. "I'll run to find out what happened. Find me on deck."

Your heart pounds as you run to the deck. It's crowded with passengers. You're baffled by what you see and hear. Officers shout for women and children to get into lifeboats. Some do as they're told. But many women refuse to get in. Some won't leave their menfolk behind. Others are terrified of being lowered into the sea in the tiny lifeboats. They think it's safer to stay on deck. Whatever has happened, they see no need to flee the unsinkable *Titanic*.

You stop a steward and ask what's happened.

"We've hit an iceberg," he replies. "Captain's ordered passengers into lifeboats, just as a precaution."

Anne reappears. "I found their mother," she says breathlessly. "What's going on?"

You tell her about the iceberg. Neither of you can believe you slept through it. But that means the damage wasn't that bad, right?

One officer calls to you and Anne.

"Will you please get into the lifeboat?" he asks, exasperated. "I'm not supposed to let employees on, but these ladies might follow your example."

You and Anne dutifully step into a lifeboat and encourage the other women to do the same. Finally, the boat is full, and the officers lower it slowly down 70 feet to the water. A few passengers row the lifeboat until it's more than a mile away from the ship.

Turn the page.

At first, you are annoyed to be in this tiny boat in the cold night air. But as it moves farther from the ship, you can see that the unimaginable is happening. The *Titanic* is tilting to one side. It's actually sinking! You and the others watch in horror as the front half of the ship is enveloped in black waves. Screams pierce the black, cold night.

"I can't look," you say, burying your head in Anne's shoulder. You hear terrible sounds of tearing metal and huge explosions. The air fills with the screams of people thrown into the water, begging for help. The horror seems to go on forever, then Anne squeezes you tightly.

"*Titanic* is gone," she whispers.

You sob into her shoulder as the screams die away into silence. You don't know how much time has passed when a passenger shouts, "There's a ship!"

You raise your head to see the *Carpathia*'s lights in the distance. You both cry from relief and from grief. The worst night of your life is finally over, but nightmares of it will haunt you until your dying day.

THE END

To follow another path, turn to page 8.
To learn what happened after *Titanic* sank, turn to page 101.

You find Joe in the galley stacking crates of fresh vegetables. He tells you that this is the galley for the first- and second-class passengers. It has the most modern improvements, such as cooking ranges that stretch for almost 100 feet and include nineteen ovens. He slips you a fresh-baked roll, still warm from the oven.

"My shift ends at 11:00," Joe says. "I know it's late, but would you like to take a walk with me before bed?" It's later than you'd prefer to stay up, but you really like Joe. You agree, happily.

At noon, the passengers arrive, and you greet them warmly. For the next four days, you work hard for the passengers under your care, cleaning, running errands, and making their voyage as pleasurable as possible. You don't stop until you fall into your bunk each night, exhausted.

You allow yourself one small pleasure each evening—a stroll with Joe along the deck. Sometimes, you see Thomas Andrews, *Titanic's* designer. He always greets you with a kind word.

It's Sunday night, and you're off duty. You meet Joe and have a lovely walk about the deck. It's very dark, and the sea is flat and calm. You're lost in conversation when a jolt startles you. You hear a low, crunching sound. The deck shakes for a few seconds. Then all is still. The engines stop.

Quickly, you and Joe rush into action.

"I'll go up to the bridge. Surely, one of the officers knows what's going on," Joe says.

"I'll check with the stewards," you reply.

Joe takes off toward the bridge. You rush inside the ship. Before you can find a steward, a passenger in her nightdress stops you.

Turn the page.

"Miss, please fetch the doctor," she asks, desperately. "My youngest has a fever."

"In a moment, ma'am. I am trying to find out what has happened to the ship," you explain.

"The ship is fine!" she insists. "My baby can't wait."

A steward appears and pulls you aside.

"We've hit an iceberg. Please get first-class women and children to the lifeboats—Captain's orders."

"I'm not going anywhere until you find the doctor!" the passenger says.

Do you do what the passenger asks or follow captain's orders?

- To search for the doctor, go to the next page.
- To help passengers to the lifeboats, turn to page 32.

"Of course," you tell the woman. "I'll be back shortly with Dr. O'Loughlin."

You speed through the ship until you reach the doctor's cabin. But when you knock, there's no answer!

You ask a steward if he's seen Dr. O'Loughlin.

"No, miss," he replies. "The doctor is usually in the first-class lounge this time of night."

The first-class lounge is ablaze with electric lights and filled with smartly dressed men talking and playing cards. No one seems concerned about the accident. You scan the faces but don't see the doctor. You ask a waiter if the doctor had been here.

He nods. "He was called to see a sick passenger in third class," he responds. "But that was some time ago."

Turn the page.

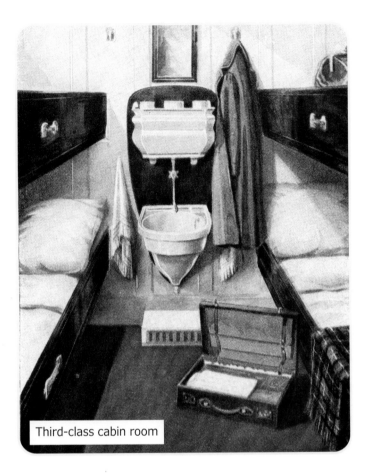

Third-class cabin room

This is getting frustrating. Should you tell the passenger that you couldn't find the doctor or take the time to search third class?

- To return to the passenger, go to the next page.
- To search for the doctor in third class, turn to page 31.

You knock on the passenger's door, and she answers.

"Where's the doctor?" she demands. Before you have a chance to explain, she throws on her coat. "I'll do it myself!" she shouts, stomping out.

"Please stay until she gets back," a young woman pleads. "I'm the nanny, and I don't know what to do."

You swallow your fear and nod. For the next hour, you and the young woman try to calm the sick baby. Finally, you hear footsteps. The doctor! You open the door to an astonished steward.

"Why are you still here?" he exclaims. "Don't you know the ship is sinking?"

You and the woman run up to the deck. It's filled with crowds of people. The woman and the baby disappear into the crowd. Thomas Andrews is standing nearby.

Turn the page.

"Not enough lifeboats," he mutters half to you and half to himself. "I told them we needed more. I can't believe this is happening . . . I'm so sorry, my dear."

A strange calm overtakes you. Your mind becomes clear even though your heart is pounding. You realize you're facing certain death. But you don't want to die in the cold. You slowly return to your cabin, climb into bed, and turn off the electric lights for the last time.

THE END

To follow another path, turn to page 8.
To learn what happened after *Titanic* sank, turn to page 101.

Dozens of people are huddled in the third-class dining saloon, speaking different languages. You struggle to find someone who understands you. Eventually, you are told that the doctor had been here but left.

It suddenly strikes you that the ship is tilting. This confirms your worst fear—*Titanic* is sinking. A group of third-class passengers are crowded in front of a door leading to the upper decks. But someone has locked it from the other side!

You run through the maze of hallways, desperately trying to find another way out. Finally, you find an unlocked door leading to the upper deck. But it's too late. Freezing sea water rushes in. Before you can even process what's happening, you are sucked into the water and drown.

THE END

To follow another path, turn to page 8.
To learn what happened after *Titanic* sank, turn to page 101.

"I'm sorry, ma'am, but I must follow captain's orders right now," you say. "I'll get you help as soon as I can." Despite what the steward said about the iceberg, you're sure there is no real danger. *Titanic* is unsinkable.

You gently wake your passengers, help them get dressed, and tie on their life belts. Finally, they're all gone, and the hallways are empty and quiet. You go back to each cabin and tidy them up, smoothing rumpled beds and turning on heaters. You want their rooms to be in order when they return.

After a while, you begin to wonder why the passengers aren't back yet. Maybe this is worse than you thought. You start to panic. You throw on a warm overcoat and dash back out onto the deck.

The deck is crowded, and there's a feeling of alarm in the air. Could the *Titanic* actually be going down?

Passengers say a tearful goodbye
before the woman is put in a lifeboat.

Turn the page.

One crewman cries, "Passengers to the lifeboats! Women and children only!" You're an employee, but your uniform can't be seen beneath your overcoat. You're desperate to get into a lifeboat. The one nearest you is full and is about to be lowered. Down the deck, crew members remove the canvas cover from another lifeboat.

There are a lot of people between you and the empty lifeboat. You might not make it in time. Do you try to get on the full lifeboat or risk squeezing through the crowds to the empty one?

- To try for the full lifeboat near you, go to the next page.
- To take your chances getting to the empty lifeboat farther away, turn to page 37.

You push through the crowd. Men are throwing deck chairs and wooden doors overboard, anything that might float. The *Titanic* really is sinking! An officer takes your arm.

"Get in!" he orders, helping you in. You spot one of the passengers you'd been caring for.

"Miss Willard!" you cry. She gives you a hug.

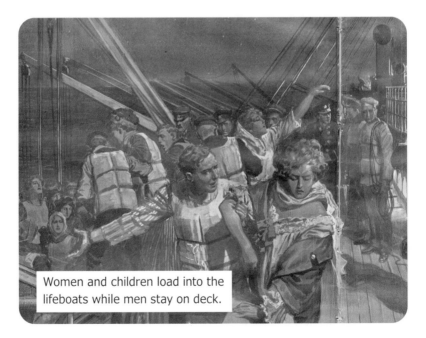

Women and children load into the lifeboats while men stay on deck.

Turn the page.

Suddenly, an officer hands you a bundle.

"Look after this, will you?" he asks.

It's a baby! The officer calls for the lifeboat to be lowered.

You're terrified as the boat creaks and sways down 70 feet to the water. The lifeboat finally hits the water with a terrible thud. The baby begins to wail as the officer in charge of the lifeboat orders that people begin rowing. Your heart breaks for the child, but you're not sure you can care for it in this stressful situation. Perhaps Miss Willard will take it if you volunteer to row.

- To offer to row, turn to page 38.
- To keep the baby in your arms, turn to page 40.

You try to push through the crowd, but you keep getting shoved back. Finally, with one mighty push, you pop out of the crowd like a cork. In front of you, John Jacob Astor is helping his young wife, Madeline, into the lifeboat. She's crying as she steps in.

At that moment, the sky lights up. It's a distress rocket! Suddenly, panic erupts on deck. The crowd surges forward, pushing you over the railing. The last thing you remember is hitting the freezing water before you disappear under the black waves.

THE END

To follow another path, turn to page 8.
To learn what happened after *Titanic* sank, turn to page 101.

You take off your coat and wrap it around the baby, then hand it to Miss Willard. Then you pick up an oar and row until your whole body is numb.

Titanic's forward is completely underwater now. One of her giant funnels breaks off and falls into the ocean with a terrifying crash, sending a wave across the water. You watch with horror as the ship breaks in two. The front half is swallowed by the sea, but the back half bobs afloat. Then it tilts forward, her great propellers rising higher into the air. The ship pauses when it's straight up and down in the water. Then with a roar *Titanic* plunges into the ocean and disappears.

It's all too much. You drop the oar and slump against Miss Willard. You're so cold, but you don't regret giving the baby the coat.

Waves of sleepiness hit you, and you can't remember why you're in this tiny boat. You begin to shiver uncontrollably. When you try to speak to Miss Willard, your words are slurred. You don't realize that these are signs that you're freezing to death.

You are dimly aware of others trying to wake you up. They know if you fall asleep, you will die. But you don't care about anything anymore. You close your eyes and drift into your final slumber.

THE END

To follow another path, turn to page 8.
To learn what happened after *Titanic* sank, turn to page 101.

You are determined to keep this baby alive. You wrap it tightly inside your coat and let other people row.

Titanic's lights glow against the night sky. You count the decks by the rows of lights on each deck. First, you count six decks above the water. When you count again, there's only five. *Titanic* is sinking—fast.

Soon, one of the enormous funnels tears away from the ship and collapses into the water with a deafening crash. The sound of people screaming overwhelms you, and you huddle your head into the baby to block the terrible sounds. After what seems like ages, someone whispers, "Merciful heavens." You hear several tremendous explosions, and you raise your head to see an incredible sight. The ship is standing straight up in the water, a black giant against the star-filled sky. Then *Titanic* slides downward, disappearing into the black sea.

You and the other survivors sit in the freezing darkness for hours. Finally, a pink glow of sunrise appears. One passenger shouts and points at a ship! You see its name—the *Carpathia*.

Eventually, several people help you onto the *Carpathia's* deck. Suddenly, a weeping woman rushes up and grabs the baby from your arms. You're shocked and happy that the baby's mother survived. You made it too. But you mourn for the good people who were lost in this terrible disaster.

THE END

To follow another path, turn to page 8.
To learn what happened after *Titanic* sank, turn to page 101.

CHAPTER 3

ALL HANDS ON DECK

You've lived a life of adventure few others can boast of. When you were only thirteen years old, you went to sea as a ship's apprentice. The sea became your home. You've survived shipwrecks, hurricanes, and raging ship fires. After all those seagoing adventures, there's nothing that scares you anymore. You love your life at sea.

Turn the page.

In 1900, you were hired by the White Star Line. You rose in the ranks to become a respected officer. You are thrilled when you learn you've been assigned to the White Star Line's new ship, the RMS *Titanic*. Its magnificence has been boasted about. It has been referred to as "the ship of dreams" and touted as unsinkable.

Titanic before setting sail

You board the ship in Belfast, Ireland, where it was built, for an inspection trip. The trip will take you to Southampton, England. There, your passengers will board. You and some other officers and crew spend several days looking over the ship's instruments, equipment, and machinery. When you arrive in Southampton, *Titanic* is almost ready for her maiden voyage.

Today is sailing day, finally. It's been a chaotic few days, but you're confident that everything will be in order for the passengers to embark this afternoon. But you've still got a few things left to check this morning.

• To assist with a lifeboat test, turn to page 46.
• To inspect the water pumps and the watertight compartments, turn to page 53.

You join several officers and about 40 crew members on the boat deck for the lifeboat test. Of course, this is unnecessary. You can't imagine the lifeboats would be needed on a ship as modern and capable as the *Titanic*. There aren't even enough lifeboats for all the passengers on board. Nevertheless, this drill must be done.

Some of the crew put on life belts. The officers choose two lifeboats, and nine men climb into each one. The rest of the crew lowers the lifeboats into the water.

The men in the lifeboats row around the harbor, testing the oars and other equipment. After a few minutes, the lifeboats are lifted back onto *Titanic*'s deck. The whole drill only lasts about 30 minutes. You sign off on the inspections.

Around noon, the passengers begin to arrive. You station yourself near the first-class entrance and warmly greet everyone. When all the passengers are on board, the great whistle blows, signaling the start of *Titanic*'s maiden voyage.

For the next four days, everything runs smoothly. By Sunday, April 14, you have things well in hand. This evening, your shift is supposed to start at 6:00 p.m. But you're feeling ill, so you ask another officer to cover for you and return to your cabin. Around 11:40, you're awakened by an odd vibration that only lasts a few seconds. You wonder if you should go back to sleep or check in at the bridge to see what happened.

- To go back to sleep, turn to page 48.
- To go to the bridge, turn to page 50.

It's probably nothing, so you fall back into a deep sleep. Much later, you are awakened by a scream coming from somewhere outside your cabin. You throw on a coat and run onto the deck. The deck is tilted, and the bow is already underwater. This can't be! The grand ship is sinking! Worse yet, all the lifeboats are gone. Hundreds of panicked passengers are scrambling to the stern, which is rising into the air.

Passengers in lifeboats watch from a distance as the grand boat sinks.

A thousand confused thoughts jumble your mind as you grasp the railing to keep your footing. What happened? Why didn't anyone wake you? Why didn't you recognize the danger earlier?

You know that no human can stay alive for long in the freezing ocean. Then your mind clears as you make a final decision. Your body shakes from fear and the cold as you climb over the rail and drop into the ocean, lost forever in a watery grave.

THE END

To follow another path, turn to page 8.
To learn what happened after *Titanic* sank, turn to page 101.

You quickly put on your uniform and go to the bridge. First Officer Murdoch is on duty.

"What happened?" you ask.

Officer Murdoch looks stricken. "At about 11:40 p.m., the lookouts sounded the warning bell. Iceberg dead ahead. I turned hard and had the engines shut down. I thought she missed the iceberg, but she struck."

"Let's hope the damage isn't too bad," you reply.

"The captain is inspecting the damage now," Officer Murdoch says.

After a time, Captain Smith appears with a large group, including Thomas Andrews, the ship's designer. You look at their faces and get a sinking feeling in your stomach. You know the worst has happened. *Titanic* will sink.

"Prepare the lifeboats," the captain orders. "Wake all the passengers and have them put on their life belts and come to the boat deck."

He pauses. Then he continues, "Women and children only."

You and the other officers instantly spring into action, pulling the covers off the lifeboats. As you work, passengers begin to arrive. You reassure them that everything's fine, even though you know the truth.

You load about twenty-eight people onto a nearby lifeboat, then stop. Although the lifeboats can hold seventy people, you're afraid the ropes won't bear the weight. Each lifeboat must have an officer in charge, so you jump in and give the order to lower. As your lifeboat touches the water, you order the passengers to row away from the ship.

Turn the page.

For the next two hours, you watch the disaster unfold before your eyes. White distress rockets light the night sky as the ship's bow is engulfed in water. With a crack and a roar, one huge funnel collapses, and the ship breaks in half! The front half disappears into the sea as the stern rises above the waves. It goes higher until it is straight up in the water. All the lights go out, and thunderous explosions rock the night as *Titanic* slides into the ocean.

Slowly, the screams from the water die down as the victims lose their fight with the freezing cold water. For the next couple of hours, you wait for rescue. Finally, you see lights in the darkness. A ship! You'll soon be safe and warm again, following the worst, most shocking disaster of your life.

THE END

To follow another path, turn to page 8.
To learn what happened after *Titanic* sank, turn to page 101.

You meet with Joseph Bell, the chief engineer. He shows you *Titanic*'s huge water pumps. They can remove 1,700 tons of water an hour!

"She'd have to be badly damaged to take on that much water," he says.

Titanic's hull is divided into 16 watertight sections with huge steel watertight doors. If the doors begin to close, an alarm bell goes off. This alerts the crew, giving them enough time to escape before the doors shut.

"I heard that the walls of the compartments don't go all the way up. Is that true?" you ask.

"Yes," he says. "If one compartment flooded all the way up, the water would spill over into the next compartment. But that's not likely with this grand ship!"

Turn the page.

Men stand next to one of *Titanic*'s propellers before the ship is launched.

Your inspections are complete. Now it's time to greet the passengers as they arrive. For the next few hours, you walk the halls, saying hello and answering any questions. When everyone is on board, you return to the bridge. You're ready to start your adventure aboard *Titanic*.

After four uneventful days, it's now Sunday, April 14. Your shift starts at 6:00 p.m. All day, other ships have sent *Titanic* reports of ice. Fortunately, most of the ice is far away. Around 9:00 p.m., Captain Smith appears on the bridge.

"Good evening," he says. "It's cold, isn't it?"

"Yes sir," you reply. "In fact, the air is only one degree above freezing."

The captain nods. "I'm sure the lookouts will spot any iceberg in plenty of time to give a warning," he says. You agree.

"If it becomes at all doubtful, let me know at once," the captain says as he leaves the bridge.

At 10:00 p.m., First Officer Murdoch arrives to relieve you. Your last duty of the evening is to go on rounds through the ship. Normally, you're anxious to be off duty, so you usually just give Officer Murdoch a brief report and start your rounds. But you're feeling conversational tonight and wouldn't mind chatting for a bit before you leave.

- To leave the bridge and begin your rounds, turn to page 56.

- To chat with Officer Murdoch before you leave, turn to page 62.

You quickly give Officer Murdoch the ice warnings and relay the captain's message. Then you head off on your rounds. During rounds, you check in with other officers and staff, make sure everyone has what they need to do their jobs, and chat with passengers. You also check in on the quartermasters. These are professional sailors who steer the ship, deliver messages, and stand as watchmen.

Officer Murdoch

You complete your rounds sometime after 11:30 p.m. As you make your way to the upper decks, the ship begins to vibrate. You hear a strange grinding noise. It sounds like a propeller is broken. Do you return to the bridge to report it to Officer Murdoch? Or do you go below to the engine room to confirm your suspicion first?

• To head toward the bridge, turn to page 58.
• To check below, turn to page 60.

You dash toward the bridge. To your surprise, the starboard deck is covered with ice. Your heart is in your throat as you peer into the dark night. Then you see the outline of an enormous iceberg! You must have hit it. You rush to the bridge.

As you turn, you trip on a piece of ice and fall, slamming your head on the deck and sliding toward the edge! Miraculously, you grab the freezing metal rail with one hand. For a moment, you dangle 70 feet above the water. Blood pours from your head wound into your eyes as you shout for help, dizzy and terrified.

Several people appear and reach for you as you try to pull yourself up. You lose your grip, falling through the freezing air. Everything goes dark, and you lose consciousness before you plunge into the sea. It's a merciful death, though it doesn't seem so at the time. Most of the other people on the ship will join you in a couple of hours. Your accident saves you the horror of going down on a sinking ship.

THE END

To follow another path, turn to page 8.
To learn what happened after *Titanic* sank, turn to page 101.

You take the crew stairs down as fast as you can. As you get closer to the boiler rooms, you hear shouting and rushing water.

A panicked crewman sees you. "One of the engineers fell and broke his leg," he says. "They took him to Boiler Room Five."

You rush to the boiler room and find Engineer Jonathan Shepherd lying on the floor. Frederick Barrett, the lead stoker, is with him.

Titanic's boiler room

"Go back to your post!" you shout to Barrett. "I'll get Shepherd to safety." Barrett nods and leaves.

You have no choice but to drag Shepherd to the door. As you grip him under the arms, the emergency alarm bells go off. The watertight doors are closing! Frantically, you pull him across the floor. You don't make it before the watertight door drops shut, trapping you both inside. You want to scream in fear and frustration! Only a few seconds more, and you both would have been saved.

Suddenly, a thunderous crash rocks the boiler room. The pressure from the water in the next compartment collapses the wall, sending a flood of freezing seawater onto your heads. You're slammed against the metal hull and crushed instantly.

THE END

To follow another path, turn to page 8.
To learn what happened after *Titanic* sank, turn to page 101.

You hand Officer Murdoch the wireless messages and tell him about the ice warnings. You also tell him that the captain wants to be called if ice is spotted.

"I can't remember a night so clear," Officer Murdoch says. "The lookouts will see an iceberg long before it becomes a danger."

"I'm sure you're right," you reply. "I don't envy the lookouts, though. It's freezing tonight."

After a few more minutes of idle chat, you say good night. You rush through your rounds and are soon in bed. Just as you're falling asleep, the ship shudders. After a few seconds, the shaking stops.

You dress quickly and go to the boat deck. You don't see anything wrong, so you make your way back to your cabin. Fourth Officer Joseph Boxhall stops you before you get there.

"We've hit an iceberg," he says quietly. "The water is up to F deck in the mail room. Captain says to start loading lifeboats as a precaution."

You're not convinced the situation is serious. You'd like to check out the damage yourself. But perhaps you should follow the captain's orders and prepare the lifeboats.

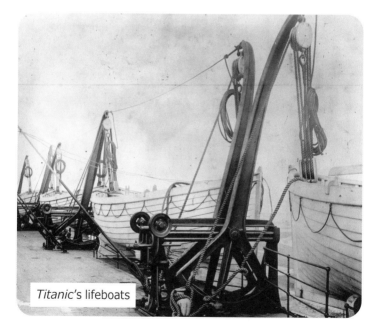
Titanic's lifeboats

- To investigate the damage, turn to page 64.
- To prepare the lifeboats, turn to page 65.

Your curiosity gets the better of you. You take the crew stairs down several decks. Then you see green seawater covering the bottom of the stairs. How deep is it, and where is it coming from?

There's only one way to find out. Your curiosity overrides your panic, and you foolishly jump into the water. It's much colder than you expected it to be! The pressure of the rushing water carries you forward, slamming you into a wall. You don't even have time to reflect on your bad decision before the life drains from you.

THE END

To follow another path, turn to page 8.
To learn what happened after *Titanic* sank, turn to page 101.

You give the order for the lifeboats to be prepared for launch. You see Captain Smith standing nearby. He has just returned from an inspection of the ship.

"Hadn't we better get the women and children in the boats, sir?" you ask. He nods absently. You can tell by the look on his face that the worst has happened. Your heart beats faster at this realization.

You call for women and children only. You refuse to let any men onto the lifeboats. After each boat leaves, you peek down an emergency crew staircase. At first, you see water far at the bottom. Each time you look, the water has risen higher. *Titanic* is going down fast.

Finally, the last lifeboat is gone. Two collapsible lifeboats are left, but they're tied down on the roof of the officer's quarters.

Turn the page.

For the last two hours, you've turned away every man who has tried to get into a lifeboat. The ship is going down quickly now. You may have just enough time to try to save yourself on one of the collapsible boats. But you don't know if you could live with yourself if you do.

Do you untie the lifeboats before the ship sinks? Or do you accept your duty and go down with the ship?

- To untie the collapsible lifeboats, go to the next page.
- To go down with the ship, turn to page 68.

You and several other men untie the first collapsible lifeboat. You fill it with as many women as you can find, then climb in and release it into the water. Just then, a wave washes overboard. You tumble into the ocean as the women on board scream. They reach for you, but the lightweight canvas boat rocks dangerously when they move.

You frantically try to grab something, but another wave carries you away. Your mind goes dark, and you sink beneath the surface forever. You can't help feeling this is the fate you deserve.

THE END

To follow another path, turn to page 8.
To learn what happened after *Titanic* sank, turn to page 101.

A huge wave rolls across the deck, washing hundreds out to sea. Fear freezes you in place for a moment. Then you shake it off. You've made the sea your life. It only fits that it would be the death of you. Bravely, you dive into the freezing Atlantic.

A strong pressure below the water pulls you under, sucking you beneath the waves. You're trapped against a wire grating that covers one of the ship's huge air shafts. You start to black out, convinced these are your last moments.

Then a blast of air escaping from deep inside the ship blows through the air shaft. It shoots you to the surface. You gulp air, shocked to be alive. Before you can move, one of ship's funnels topples into the ocean, causing a huge wave that flings you away from the sinking ship.

When you come up for air, you see *Titanic's* stern rising until the ship is standing completely straight up in the water. Loud booms and crashes shake the air as her lights finally go out, and she slides headfirst into the sea.

There are about 30 men around you. Some are standing on the bottom of an upturned collapsible boat. Others are in the water, hanging on to the edge of it. You scramble onto the boat. You want to save as many lives as you can! You could pull other survivors onto the overturned lifeboat. But the more people climb on it, the more likely it is to sink. Perhaps you should direct the survivors on the raft how to keep the lightweight boat afloat.

• To pull survivors out of the water, turn to page 70.
• To organize the survivors on the upturned boat, turn to page 71.

You reach out to someone holding onto the side of the boat. As he reaches out to you, a wave pulls him away. You try again and manage to get a hold of another man. In a panic, he pulls you into the ocean! He pushes you under and won't let go. After a moment or two, you slowly sink beneath the waves.

THE END

To follow another path, turn to page 8.
To learn what happened after *Titanic* sank, turn to page 101.

Keeping this raft afloat will take the effort of all on board. You order everyone to stand up and face one direction.

As the ocean pitches and rolls the wooden raft-like boat, you shout, "Lean right! Lean left! Stand straight!" This keeps the boat balanced on the waves.

The freezing weather is too much for many men. One by one, they slip into the sea.

Somehow, you and several others manage to stay on your feet through the night. But the collapsible boat is slowly sinking. When the sun rises, you and the others are up to your knees in water.

You spot a ship on the horizon! You also see several lifeboats nearby. You shout, but no one in the lifeboats can hear you.

Turn the page.

Then you remember the officer's whistle in your pocket. By some miracle, it's still there! A loud blast of the whistle gets their attention. Immediately, two lifeboats come. The men on the collapsible boat gratefully climb in. As you watch the *Carpathia* steam closer, you can't believe you survived.

THE END

To follow another path, turn to page 8.
To learn what happened after *Titanic* sank, turn to page 101.

CHAPTER 4

EVERY MAN FOR HIMSELF

You've enjoyed a quiet life, growing up in the English countryside. You went to university and became a science teacher. But lately, you've been feeling restless. Maybe it's time for a little adventure! You decide to tour the United States. You purchase a second-class ticket on the ship everyone is talking about—the *Titanic*. It's exciting to be traveling on a ship during her maiden voyage. You've also heard that *Titanic* is more luxurious than any other ship.

Turn the page.

The night before the voyage begins, you stay in a nice hotel near the Southampton docks. At breakfast the next morning, you can see the huge funnels of the ship rising above the rooftops of town. Two friends join you for breakfast to see you off. They beg you to take them on board for a peek before she sails.

It's a few hours before official boarding, but a kind crewman lets your group onto the ship. You could explore the first-class areas. Or you could take a look at the second-class accommodations where you'll be staying.

- To go to first class, go to the next page.
- To explore the second-class areas, turn to page 81.

Your group wanders through the first-class libraries, lounges, and dining saloon. It is all so elegant. Up on the boat deck, you find the first-class gymnasium. You and your friend climb onto the stationary bicycles as a crowd of newspaper photographers enter. You and your friend smile for the cameras!

Nearby is the wireless room. Wireless technology is new and exciting! You peek in and a young man greets you, "I'm Harold Bride," he says. "I'm the junior wireless operator on the ship. Would you like to see the wireless room?"

Mr. Bride shows you wires, machines, and brass instruments. He explains that wireless machines work by sending radio signals that are picked up by other wireless machines. Ships send iceberg warnings to each other using wireless technology.

Turn the page.

Wireless operator on board the *Titanic*

"But I expect most of my job will be sending personal messages from the passengers telling friends and family about *Titanic*," he says.

Suddenly, you hear *Titanic*'s whistle, signaling that official boarding is to begin. You thank Mr. Bride and say goodbye to your friends and settle in for your ocean adventure.

You're four days into your voyage and enjoying it greatly. You spend a lot of time in the second-class library, conversing with your fellow passengers. They include Reverend Ernest Carter and Mrs. Nellie Becker and her children Ruth, Marion, and baby Richard.

It's Sunday, April 14. Despite feeling a head cold coming on, you've spent another pleasant afternoon in the library. Dinner is excellent, as usual. Tonight's menu includes baked haddock, curried chicken and rice, lamb with mint sauce, roast turkey, green peas, turnips, and roast potatoes. For dessert, you choose from plum pudding, ice cream, fruit, cheese, and coffee.

Afterward, Reverend Carter leads a service. About 100 passengers arrive to sing hymns. Around 10:00 p.m., stewards put out refreshments and coffee. You all say good night around 11:00.

Turn the page.

As you get comfortable in your bed, the mattress vibrates slightly. The engines stop a few minutes later. You throw on a thin robe and go upstairs to the deck. You spot a steward leaning against a doorway.

"Why have the engines stopped?" you ask.

The steward shrugs. "I wouldn't worry too much."

Should you return to your cabin, or ask around for more information?

- To go back to your cabin, turn to page 91.
- To get more information, turn to page 93.

The second-class areas are as impressive as first-class ones on other ships. They are filled with rich carpets, beautiful furniture, and expensive decorations. The library is especially elegant, with comfortable armchairs and writing tables spread out around the room.

As you wander around the second-class deck, you pass the lifeboats.

"It's a pity those lifeboats take up so much deck space," one of your friends remarks. "They certainly spoil the ocean view, don't they?"

You agree. Who needs lifeboats on an unsinkable ship?

Around noon, the ship's whistle blows to signal the ship is about to leave. Your friends thank you for this exciting adventure exploring *Titanic* before stepping off the ship.

Turn the page.

For the next four days at sea, you enjoy sleeping in and eating wonderful food on this amazing ship. You spend time meeting many of your fellow second-class passengers, such as Reverend Ernest Carter and his wife, Lillian. You also meet Mrs. Nellie Becker and her three children, Ruth, Marion, and baby Richard.

Sunday, April 14, is another lovely day. The weather is clear but cold. You spend the afternoon in the library, but by evening, you begin to feel unwell.

"You don't look good, my boy," Reverend Carter remarks. "Here," he says, pulling a small packet of powder from his jacket pocket. "It's medicine. Another passenger gave it to me. Kicked my cold in a few days."

Finally, you excuse yourself and head back to your cabin. All you need is a good night's sleep. The medicine could help. But you're not sure you're sick enough for it. Maybe you can sleep it off without it.

• To take the medicine, go to the next page.
• To have some tea, turn to page 84.

You swallow the medicine, hoping to feel better in the morning. It completely knocks you out. You don't wake when *Titanic* hits the iceberg. You're not roused by stewards knocking on your door or the commotion in the hallway. You lie fast asleep as *Titanic* sinks, taking you to the bottom of the ocean.

It is a merciful death, as your chances of escape would not have been great. Only twenty percent of the men aboard the ship survived.

THE END

To follow another path, turn to page 8.
To learn what happened after *Titanic* sank, turn to page 101.

You climb into bed with a cup of tea and a book. Finally, you turn out the electric light and fall into a deep sleep.

Hours later, you sit bolt upright, confused as to what awakened you. You open the door. The hallway is filled with passengers all speaking at once. A tinge of panic washes over you. You stop an officer.

"What is going on?" you ask.

"We've hit an iceberg. All passengers to the boat deck," he says.

This is bad news, indeed. But you're sure everything will be fine. This is probably just a precautionary measure. You grab warm clothing and go onto the boat deck. There, crewmen are loading the lifeboats. "Women and children only!" they shout.

Women and children are lowered into lifeboats.

"Well, that's it then," a well-dressed man in the crowd says. "Let's head inside, chaps. No use freezing out here."

Turn the page.

The other men make their way inside. They're either not worried or very good at hiding it. You're not quite sure what to do or how dangerous this situation is.

A man standing near you whispers in your ear. "I hear they're letting men onto the boats on the portside of the ship," he says.

Do you take a chance on finding a lifeboat on the other side of the boat, or wait out the calamity inside, where it's bright and warm?

- To take a chance on a lifeboat, go to the next page.
- To go inside, turn to page 88.

You make it to the portside just as the last lifeboat is lowered. You're paralyzed with fear as seawater rises to the deck. The *Titanic* really is going down! Suddenly, a man shouts, "Don't just stand here! Find something that'll float!"

You snap out of it and grab a deck chair, gripping it as another wave carries you out to sea. The freezing water knocks your breath away. Gasping, you hang onto the chair, hoping rescue will come soon.

It's not long before you can't feel your body. You wonder if America is as wonderful as you imagined it to be when you planned your holiday trip. You close your eyes and fall unconscious. You freeze to death in your sleep, another victim of this terrible disaster.

THE END

To follow another path, turn to page 8.
To learn what happened after *Titanic* sank, turn to page 101.

You follow the group inside. Suddenly, Mrs. Becker's 12-year-old daughter, Ruth, appears!

"Sir, I can't find my mother! Can you help me?"

Quickly, you take Ruth to the boat deck. There's a commotion at the rail. It's Ruth's mother, Nellie, being pushed into a lifeboat. Ruth sees her at the last minute.

"Mother!" Ruth cries.

Nellie sees Ruth and screams, "Oh, Ruth! Thank heavens! Get into the next boat!"

Ruth runs to the next lifeboat, and the officer lifts her in. He calls for more women and children, but no one steps forward. Then he points at you.

"Get in," he says curtly.

You jump into the boat, and the officer orders it to be lowered. When it's safely down, you grab an oar along with several others and begin rowing away from the ship. You watch in horror as the bow of *Titanic* sinks underwater, and the stern tilts higher.

You can't believe what you're seeing. Doomed passengers frantically climb up and away from the oncoming sea. Ruth begins crying as explosions rock the ship. Without warning, one large funnel collapses into the water with a crash.

The sound of people screaming fills the air as the ship breaks in two, sending the bow into the sea. The stern continues to rise until the enormous propellers are high in the air. The lights flicker out, and *Titanic* sinks into the ocean.

Turn the page.

All you can do is comfort Ruth and wait.
As the sun rises, you see a ship! It's the *Carpathia*.
One by one, the survivors are lifted onto the ship.

You hear a familiar voice shouting, "Ruth! Ruth! Has anyone seen my girl?"

"Mama!" Ruth screams. Mrs. Becker runs across the deck as Ruth jumps into her arms. You and many other passengers weep at this emotional reunion. You think of the men you followed into the ship. If not for Ruth, you would be at the bottom of the ocean with them instead of here, alive.

THE END

To follow another path, turn to page 8.
To learn what happened after *Titanic* sank, turn to page 101.

You climb into your still-warm bed and fall asleep. Hours later, you're awakened by a loud booming noise. Your heart pounds as you dress quickly. You burst out into the hall, expecting to see other frightened passengers. Instead, the brightly lit hallway is empty and silent. Several cabin doors stand eerily open. What's happening?

You get to the boat deck. It's chaos everywhere. Crowds of passengers rush toward the stern. You join them, wondering why you can't walk straight. You are shocked when you realize that the deck is tilting downward toward the bow. Waves roll over the foredeck. *Titanic* is sinking!

You run wildly from one side of the ship to the other and see that all the lifeboats are gone. Suddenly, the screech of tearing metal rips through the air.

Turn the page.

You look up as one of the huge funnels sways. It begins to fall right above you! You dive into the water, hoping to escape, but you're quickly crushed by the falling funnel. You die in this terrible disaster, along with more than 1,500 other people.

THE END

To follow another path, turn to page 8.
To learn what happened after *Titanic* sank, turn to page 101.

You find a steward who is knocking on cabin doors and calling for passengers to wake up.

"What has happened?" you ask him. "Is it serious?"

"We hit an iceberg, sir," he replies. "If I were you, I'd get to a lifeboat."

Quickly, you return to your cabin to get dressed and tie on your life belt. When you reach the deck, all the lifeboats on this side are gone. A sick fear grips you.

Suddenly, you hear a voice from below, shouting, "Any more ladies?"

You peer over the railing where a lifeboat has just been launched. The crewman looks up and sees you.

"Are there any ladies up there?"

"No," you call.

Turn the page.

"Jump in if you dare," the crewman yells.

This may be your only chance to escape a sinking ship. You throw your legs over the rail and jump, landing in the lifeboat. The crewman in charge yells, "Lower the boat!"

It seems like forever before the lifeboat finally touches the water. Then you look up to see another lifeboat being lowered right on top of you! Your lifeboat is still attached to its ropes, so it can't move. You and the other passengers shout a warning, but the lifeboat keeps coming down!

One crewman pulls out a knife and begins to cut the ropes of your lifeboat. You remember that you also have a small knife in your pocket. Do you help the crewman cut the ropes or join the other passengers in pushing away the oncoming lifeboat?

- To help cut the ropes, turn to page 96.
- To push your lifeboat out of the way, turn to page 99.

One lifeboat is lowered on top of another.

Quickly, you pull out your knife and saw at the ropes. Your lifeboat breaks away just as the one above it drops into the exact spot you were in! Two passengers row the boat to safety with great speed.

Suddenly, an explosion rocks the great ship, and a funnel collapses into the water with a horrific crash! More explosions are followed by the ship breaking in half. The bow slides into the water as the stern begins to tilt upward, climbing higher until the section is standing straight up. *Titanic* pauses there as crashes and explosions fill the air. Then she plunges into the sea, disappearing forever.

For the next hour or so, you and the other survivors wait for rescue. You strain your eyes against the blackness, hoping to see a ship's lights. Finally, you do! When dawn arrives, you see the ship's name—*Carpathia*.

The *Carpathia*

One by one, the survivors are lifted onto the ship. The *Carpathia*'s crew are waiting with warm blankets and food for all of you.

"Search the area for more survivors!" Captain Rostron orders. For several hours, the *Carpathia* circles the area, but there is no one else to save. You're heartbroken at the great loss of life.

Turn the page.

As you gaze out at the ocean, someone taps your shoulder. It's your friend Mrs. Becker!

"Have you seen my Ruth?" she asks frantically. "Do you know where she is?"

Your heart sinks. You're about to answer her that you haven't seen Ruth, but a screech interrupts your reply. Ruth runs across the deck yelling, "Mama!"

Mrs. Becker bursts into tears as her daughter jumps into her arms. Tears of happiness blur your vision as you watch this miraculous reunion. But with happiness, comes grief at the hundreds of others who perished in this terrible disaster.

THE END

To follow another path, turn to page 8.
To learn what happened after *Titanic* sank, turn to page 101.

"Heave!" you shout, pushing against the bottom of the lifeboat above. You think it's working! As you push again, the lifeboat above knocks you into the water. You're caught between the lifeboat and the hull of *Titanic*. Just then, a wave slams the lifeboat against the giant ship, crushing you between them. You were so close to surviving. But in the end, you're just another casualty in what will become a historic disaster.

THE END

To follow another path, turn to page 8.
To learn what happened after *Titanic* sank, turn to page 101.

CHAPTER 5

AFTER THE DISASTER

Of the ships that might have heard *Titanic*'s frantic distress calls, the *Carpathia* was the first to respond. Her captain, Arthur Rostron, assumed *Titanic* would still be afloat when he arrived. He prepared his ship for what he thought would be a rescue of more than 2,000 people. Instead, all he found were about 700 survivors in lifeboats.

Four days later, on April 18, the *Carpathia* arrived in New York City. There were joyful meetings as survivors reunited with their families. Other people broke down in despair when their loved ones never appeared.

One survivor, Violet Jessop, was a first-class stewardess. After the disaster, Violet worked on other White Star Line ships. She also served as a Red Cross nurse during World War I (1914–1918). In 1916, she survived a second ship disaster, the sinking of the *Britannic*. She went on to work at sea for 40 years. Violet Jessop died in 1971 at the age of 83.

Second Officer Charles Lightoller was the most senior officer to survive the sinking. On that night, he was in charge of filling lifeboats. When all were full, he jumped into the water and survived by climbing onto a collapsible lifeboat.

After the *Titanic* disaster, Lightoller joined the British Royal Navy during World War I. During World War II (1939–1945), he volunteered the use of his own boat to the Royal Navy. Lightoller was 78 when he died in 1952.

Survivor Lawrence Beesley boarded *Titanic* as a second-class passenger. As his lifeboat was lowered into the ocean, another one was coming down on top of them. Luckily, a crewman was able to cut the ropes, freeing the lifeboat before it was crushed. After the disaster, Beesley returned to England and published the first book about the disaster, *The Loss of the S.S.* Titanic. He died in 1967 at the age of 89.

Investigations into the disaster began the day after the *Carpathia* arrived in New York. These hearings uncovered many mistakes that led to the sinking. As a result, laws and regulations were passed to make sea travel safer.

The worst mistake was that *Titanic* did not have enough lifeboats for all the people on board. The designers did not want lifeboats crowding the decks. Had they all been full, the ship's lifeboats could have held 1,178 people. But there were 2,222 people on *Titanic.* A new law required all ships to have enough lifeboats for everyone on board.

Another fatal mistake was that the watertight compartment walls did not go all the way up to the lower decks. This allowed water to spill over into adjacent compartments and sink the ship. Because of the disaster, today's ships are designed so that watertight compartments are better sealed on all sides and the tops reach the decks above.

Titanic sank more than 100 years ago. But the story of the disaster and the people who were on it has lived on. Now, you have a glimpse into what they went through on that fateful journey.

A crowd in New York awaits the *Carpathia's* arrival to meet the survivors of the *Titanic*.

Titanic Timeline

March 31: *Titanic* is complete and ready for her maiden voyage.

April 10: Passengers board and *Titanic* sets sail.

The *Titanic* at sea

April 14

9:00 a.m.-1:45 p.m.: *Titanic* receives multiple ice warnings from ships in the area.

7:30 p.m.: Three more ice warnings are delivered to the bridge.

11:40 p.m.: Lookouts spot an iceberg ahead and sound an alarm. The ship glances off the iceberg, causing tears in the hull below the waterline. Five watertight compartments begin to flood.

April 15

12:00 a.m. Captain Smith orders a distress call to be sent.

12:05 a.m.: The captain orders all passengers into their life belts and to assemble on deck.

12:20 a.m.: The lifeboats begin to be loaded with women and children.

12:25 a.m.: The *Carpathia* receives *Titanic*'s distress call.

12:45 a.m. to 2:05 a.m.: Lifeboats are loaded and lowered.

2:20 a.m.: *Titanic* breaks into two pieces and sinks.

4:10 a.m.: The *Carpathia* reaches the survivors.

April 18: The *Carpathia* arrives in New York with about 700 survivors.

Other Paths to Explore

1. Captain Smith was on his final voyage when he piloted the *Titanic*. As a seaman, he knew that when a ship was sinking the captain should be the last person off the ship. What thoughts do you think were running through his mind when he realized the ship was going down before help could arrive for everyone?

2. Imagine being a third-class passenger on *Titanic*. Gates on the stairs separated third class from the rest of the ship. You could be punished for stepping foot in any "upper-class" areas. When the ship hit the iceberg, officers barricaded doors and stairwells to keep third-class passengers belowdecks. Do you think that was the right call? Why or why not? What might the third-class passengers have felt in that moment?

3. The new laws passed after the *Titanic* sank saved many lives. But they weren't good news for everyone. Imagine you own a small shipping business. New lifeboats, more crew, and adding a stronger hull to your ships will cost you a lot of money! How might you feel about these changes, and what might you do about it?

Bibliography

Beesley, Lawrence. *Loss of the SS* Titanic
public-library.uk/ebooks/58/74.pdf

Butler, Daniel Allen. *Unsinkable: The Full Story of the RMS*
Titanic. New York: Da Capo Press, 2002.

Violet Constance Jessop
encyclopedia-titanica.org/titanic-survivor/violet-constance-
jessop.html

Lightoller, Charles, Titanic *and Other Ships*
gutenberg.net.au/ebooks03/0301011h.html

Lord, Walter. *The Night Lives On.* New York: Jove Books,
1986.

Encyclopedia Titanica
encyclopedia-Titanica.org

Titanic *Inquiry Project*
Titanicinquiry.org

Glossary

adjacent (uh-JAY-suhnt)—nearby or next to

bow (BOU)—the front end of a boat

foredeck (FORE-dek)—the front-most deck on a ship with several decks

hull (HUHL)—the main body of a ship, which makes it float

portside (PORT-side)—the left side of a ship looking forward

saloon (suh-LOON)—a large space for the common use of passengers on a ship

starboard (STAR-burd)—the right-hand side of a ship looking forward

stern (STURN)—the back end of a ship

stoker (STOH-kuhr)—a crewmember in charge of tending a ship's boilers

Read More

Anastasia, Laura McClure. *Four Days on the* Titanic.
New York: Children's Press, 2022.

Eyewitness Titanic. New York: DK Press, 2021.

Halls, Kelly Milner. *The Mystery of the* Titanic: *A Historical
Investigation for Kids*. New York: Rockridge Press, 2021.

Internet Sites

DK Find Out: The Titanic
dkfindout.com/us/history/titanic/

Kids Discover Online: Titanic
online.kidsdiscover.com/unit/Titanic

National Geographic for Kids: Remembering the Titanic
kids.nationalgeographic.com/history/article/a-titanic-
anniversary

Time for Kids: On Board the Titanic
timeforkids.com/k1/on-board-Titanic-2/

JOIN OTHER HISTORICAL ADVENTURES WITH MORE
YOU CHOOSE SEEKING HISTORY!

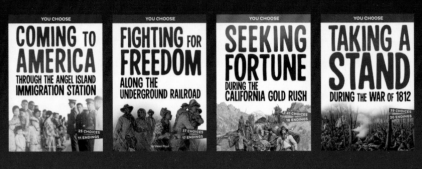

About the Author

Allison Lassieur is an award-winning author of more than 150 history and nonfiction books about everything from Ancient Rome to the International Space Station. Her books have received several *Kirkus* starred reviews and *Booklist* recommendations, and her historical novel *Journey to a Promised Land* was awarded the 2020 Kansas Library Association Notable Book Award, and Library of Congress Great Reads Book selection. Allison lives in upstate New York with her husband, daughter, a scruffy, loveable mutt named Jingle Jack, and more books than she can count.